IDENTIFYING ARCHITECTURE

The Diagram Group

BROCKHAMPTON
DIAGRAM
GUIDES

Identifying Architecture

First published in Great Britain in 1997 by
Brockhampton Press Ltd
20 Bloomsbury Street
London
WC1 2QA
a member of the Hodder Headline Group PLC

ISBN 1-86019-747-7

Also in this series:
Calligraphy
Card Games
How the Body Works
Kings and Queens of Britain
Magic Tricks
Party Games
Soccer Skills

Introduction

Identifying Architecture is an introduction to different types of buildings, architectural styles and the most common and interesting features of a range of British buildings. The first two sections of the book describe styles of architecture in Britain from Classical times to the Modern Age. The second to fifth sections are filled with descriptions and diagrams to help you identify classical features, Georgian and Victorian houses, styles of church architecture and the different parts of a castle. The final section illustrates some of the many unusual buildings to be found throughout Britain.

Contents

Architectural periods

12000–3000 BC	Mesolithic Age (Middle Stone Age)
3000–1800 BC	Neolithic Age (New Stone Age)
1800–550 BC	Bronze Age
550 BC–AD 43	Iron Age
43–400	Roman
400–650	Dark Ages
650–1066	Anglo-Saxon
1066–1189	Norman
1189–1307	Early-English
1307–1350	Decorated
1327–1520	Perpendicular
1520–1558	Tudor
1558–1603	Elizabethan
1603–1625	Jacobean
1625–1689	Stuart
1689–1714	Queen Anne (Baroque)
1714–1830	Georgian
1810–1830	Regency (Late Georgian)
1837–1901	Victorian
1901–1914	Edwardian
1922–present	International Style (Modern)

Architectural styles

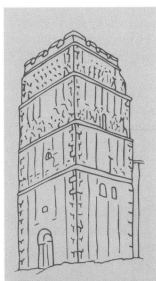

Anglo-Saxon church tower; Earls Barton, c. 1000

19th-century **Classical** facade; The Tate Gallery London, 1897

Anglo-Saxon Most buildings were of wood and have disappeared. Some simple stone churches survive.

Art Deco A 1920s and 1930s style, characterized by geometrical shapes, stylized natural forms and symmetrical designs.

Art Nouveau From the 1880s to the early 1900s architects such as Charles Rennie Mackintosh adapted sinuous natural forms and applied them to *objet d'art*, costumes, and the shapes of windows, doors and mouldings.

Arts and Crafts A 19th-century style of design, inspired by, and applied to, everyday objects; it stressed medieval styles and manual skills as a reaction against industrialization.

Baroque A European style, confined to churches and palaces, in which Classical forms and motifs were transformed by the inventive use of space and decoration.

Classical Having plans, details and facades based upon Greco-Roman styles. Common from the 16th century right up to the present day.

Decorated Second phase of the English Gothic style.

Early-English A development from Norman architecture in which Norman techniques were refined to produce the first Gothic elements.

Elizabethan The Renaissance style as

Georgian mansion;
Stoneleigh Abbey,
Warwickshire, 1726

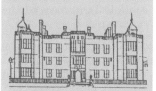

Jacobean mansion;
Charlton House,
Kent, 1612

Norman fortifications; White
Tower, Tower of London,
c. 1097

developed in England during the reign of Elizabeth I.

Georgian The British refinement of Renaissance ideals, which had themselves adapted Classical criteria. It was prevalent during the reigns of the Georges.

Gothic Originated in Europe and thrived from the late 12th to the early 16th centuries. Most expressive in churches. It is characterized by pointed arches.

Gothic Revival A 19th-century attempt to apply the ornament and aspirations of the Gothic architects.

Greek Revival A competitor to the Gothic revival. An attempt by 18th- and 19th-century architects to echo the simple purity of Greek temples.

International Style Influenced by the German Bauhaus school of architecture. It is characterized by undecorated rectangular forms and typified by high-rise buildings.

Jacobean Named after James I, it was the flowering of the Elizabethan Renaissance style. It featured Classical details grafted onto medieval-style buildings.

Modern Many modern buildings are based on the Bauhaus-derived International Style.

Neo-Classical An 18th- and 19th-century Classical style which attempted to achieve a balance of simple shapes and masses.

Norman The British Romanesque style

**Perpendicular Gothic;
West front of Winchester
Cathedral, 1367–1404**

**Tudor palace; Hampton
Court, London, c. 1520**

introduced from Normandy after the conquest of 1066.

Perpendicular The final phase in British Gothic architecture. Ever greater skill in stone building techniques produced increasingly refined structures.

Queen Anne See Baroque. This style included the use of intricate brickwork in domestic architecture.

Regency Like Neo-Classicism, this was a Classically influenced style, normally characterized by a restrained simplicity.

Renaissance In British architecture this refers to the rediscovery of ancient Classical forms and building details that took place between the early 16th and early 19th centuries.

Stuart A largely domestic architecture making use of semi-Classical forms and Dutch influences.

Transitional Of buildings containing earlier Norman elements, but which are developing towards the Gothic.

Tudor The transitional stage between the Gothic and Renaissance styles. Dominated during the reign of Henry VII.

Victorian Architecture partly associated with the Gothic revival but also incorporating much later Classical work. It was often based on Italian and French architecture and sometimes featured extensive use of cast iron.

Classical monuments

FEATURES

Architrave The lowest of the three divisions of a beam, or entablature.

Atlanta Greek name for a carved male figure used as a decorative support in Classical and Baroque architecture (**1**).

Base The lowest visible part of a building, or of an architectural or ornamental feature.

Capital The architectural feature at the top of a column.

Caryatid A sculpted female figure used as a column, most famously in the porch of the Erechtheum in Athens (**2**).

Column An upright cylindrical support.

Cornice The upper, projecting part of an entablature.

Entablature The upper part of an order of architecture, or visual beam, comprising the cornice, frieze and architrave.

Fluted column A column with deep vertical grooves.

Frieze The middle section of an entablature; or an ornamental band (with either abstract, botanical or figurative decoration) around the upper walls of a room below the cornice.

Pedestal The support on which a column stands.

Pediment A low-pitched triangular gable above a temple facade; or a smaller version of the same above a door or window.

Plinth The base of a wall or a column pedestal.

Rusticated column A ringed or banded column.

Shaft The main cylinder of a column; or a small column attached to a pillar or pier.

Volute The spiral, scroll-like form carved on the capital of an Ionic column.

Facade features
1 Pediment
2 Cornice entablature
3 Frieze entablature
4 Architrave entablature
5 Capital
6 Column

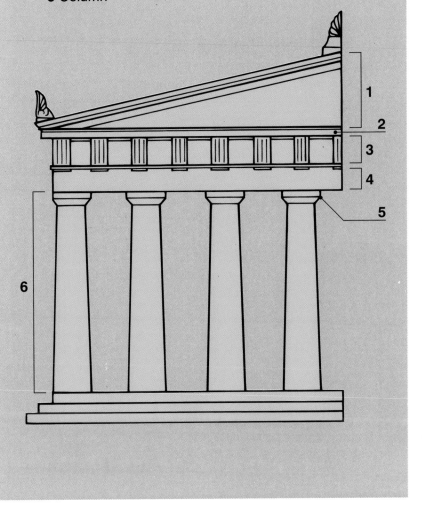

CLASSICAL ORDERS

In Classical architecture there are six standard styles of base, column, capital and entablature: Doric, Ionic, Corinthian, Tuscan, Doric Roman and composite.

Classical orders
1 Doric
2 Ionic
3 Corinthian

Derived orders
4 Tuscan
5 Doric Roman
6 Composite

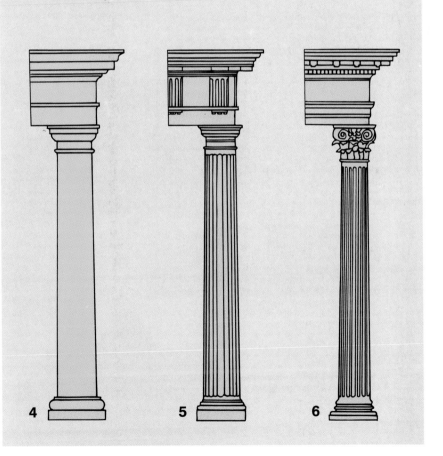

Houses

TYPES OF HOUSES

Bastel house A home in which the residential quarters are above livestock shelter and storage space (**1**).
Black house A long, single-storey, turf or straw-roofed cottage with dry-stone walls (**2**).
Bungalow A one-storey house. Traditionally with overhanging eaves.
Chalet A Swiss-style cottage or bungalow made of wood (**3**).
Chateau A grand, decorative house in the French style (**4**).

Cobbled house A round house with dry-stone walls and a domed roof (**5**).

Cottage Any small house.

Council house Low cost housing, built since 1919 and funded by municipal authorities.

Croft Another term for 'small-holding'.

Lodge Not necessarily residential; often for hunting parties. Also used to describe the gatehouse on an estate.

Longhouse A one-storey building with residents and livestock under one continuous roof (**6**).

Manor house Usually of medieval origins; traditionally the home of a local landowner or feudal lord.

Manse A house provided for the clergy.

Semi-detached Two houses joined to form one building.

Tenement A large house or building divided into rooms or flats, usually for separate rental.

Terraced A row of connected houses originating in the design of 18th-century town developments.

BUILDING MATERIALS

Brick Widely used in houses built during and after the 17th century (**1**).

Cob Damp clay mixed with chopped straw and small stones. A west country building technique (**2**).

Concrete Cast forms set onto metal frameworks or slabs which are internally re-inforced with iron rods (**3**).

Flint Small, hard round stones set into mortar (**4**). A traditional technique used where flint nodules abound in chalk landscapes.

Stone Either irregular stones (**5**) or rows of regular cut blocks (known as dressed stone) (**6**).

Tiles Timber-framed buildings with a covering of wood or clay tiles (**7**).

Timber Very often used in buildings constructed before the 18th century (**8**). Usually a strong wooden frame with plaster or brick infilling.

1

2

4

3

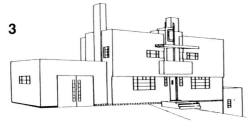

6

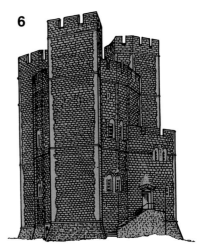

5

7

8

GEORGIAN HOUSES

Georgian houses in Britain were built during the reigns of the Kings George I, II, III and IV, between 1714 and 1830. The style was influenced by the revival of Classical Roman architecture by the Italian architect Andrea Palladio. Features of Georgian design include symmetry, simplicity and classical details such as columns. A good example of Georgian architecture appears in the regular and symmetrical design of the crescents of fine terraced houses in Bath.

A Georgian mansion

18th-century crescent, Bath

A Georgian town house

Features of Georgian houses

1 Columns Inspired by Classical design, Georgian architects made use of all three Classical orders: Doric (**a**), Ionic (**b**) and Corinthian (**c**).

2 Doors The panelled front doors are large, with columns or decoration either side and a semi-circular window (known as a fanlight) above.

3 Windows Sash windows, introduced in the early 18th century, are tall and well proportioned. They have delicate wooden glazing bars and the panes of glass are all the same size.

VICTORIAN HOUSES

Victorian houses are those built during the reign of
Queen Victoria (1837–1901). Large country houses were
built in styles revived from earlier times. For example,
Osborne House (**1**), Queen Victoria's home on the Isle of
Wight, was inspired by the Classical features of Italian
Renaissance architecture; Scarisbrick Hall in Lancashire
(**2**) has the pointed arches and rich ornamentation of
Gothic architecture; Mentmore Towers in
Buckinghamshire (**3**) has the varied skyline and large,
multi-paned rectangular windows of Elizabethan
architecture.

Much of the domestic housing built during Victoria's reign was modest and terraced or semi-detached. Many houses were built by speculative builders.

Typical Victorian terrace houses

Churches

CHURCH STYLES

Anglo-Saxon (650–11th century) Most early buildings in this style were of wood and have not survived. Saxon-style towers with pilaster stripes were still being produced after the Norman conquest.

Norman (1066–1189) The English name for Romanesque architecture (**1**), the first example of which was King Edward the Confessor's Westminster Abbey (1065). The style became dominant following the victory of William the Conqueror the following year.

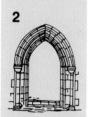

Gothic (1189–1520) Term for three periods of English architecture:

Early-English (1189–1307) The first style of English Gothic architecture (**2**). Although French in origin its ground plans, decorations, and elevations are specifically English in style.

Decorated style (1307–1350) The second distinct phase of English Gothic architecture. Simple geometrical forms, conventional yet fresh foliage carvings and the ogee arch (pointed arch with S-shaped curves on both sides) are typical characteristics (**3**).

Perpendicular (1327–1520) The third English Gothic style (**4**). Characterized by an emphasis on horizontals and verticals, large windows, lierne vaults (with secondary ribs connecting primary ribs) and (later) fan vaults. It reached its height with buildings such as King's College Chapel, Cambridge (1446–1515).

ANGLO-SAXON CHURCHES

Saxon churches were built between 650 and 1066 (the year of the Norman conquest of Britain). Most were built between 650 and 800, a period of comparative stability, but many of these were later destroyed by invading Danes. All of the surviving Saxon churches are small and of the simplest design.

Features

Corner stones Use of alternate vertical and horizontal stones at the corners (**1**).

Exterior decoration Sometimes included a criss-cross pattern of long, thin stones in the wall face.

Tower The main feature of Saxon churches (**2**).

Walls Very thick, constructed with stone facings and a rubble core.

Windows Small, with round arches (**3**).

1

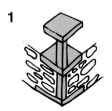

3

2

© DIAGRAM

NORMAN CHURCHES

When the Normans invaded and conquered Britain in 1066 they brought the Romanesque style with them. Their skills as masons and engineers were demonstrated in their massive, solidly-constructed churches and cathedrals. They had perfected the roof-covering technique of vaulting developed 1,000 years earlier by the Romans. This involved the use of semicircular stone arches extending the length of the roof space to form a barrel vault.

Features

1 Walls Thick, with large smooth-faced, rectangular dressed stones and an infilling of small stones. Broad buttresses support the walls.

2 Windows Narrow and semicircular.

3 Doors Surrounded by semicircular arches, often colourfully decorated with a zigzag and dog-tooth pattern.

4 Capitals Either square with cushion-type decoration, or circular.

5 Columns Massive circular structures, sometimes covered with ascending spirals or diamonds.

6 Bases Circular and set on square footings.

7 Mouldings Appeared in the following geometric styles: (**a**) chevron or zigzag; (**b**) billet.

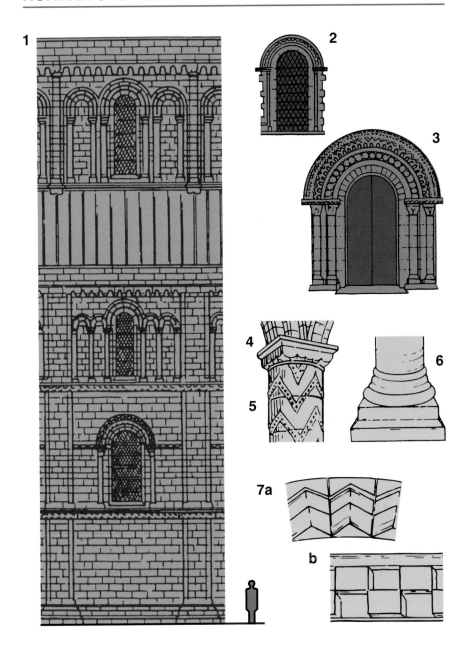

GOTHIC CHURCHES

The Gothic style dominated British architecture from the 12th to the 16th centuries. It is characterized by the use of the pointed arch, the rib vault and the flying buttress. It is a style most noted for its church architecture in which space and light are achieved through a mixture of skeletal structures, ever larger windows, vaulting and the transference of weight via ribs and buttresses.

Features

1 Boss An ornamental stone or wood block usually decorating the crossing points of a vaulted ceiling.

2 Buttress Masonry support along the side of a wall.

3 Clerestory Row of windows above the roof of the side aisles.

4 Finial Carved ornamental foliage on the top of a pinnacle or spire.

5 Flying buttress Masonry support buttress which is arched so that its base is away from the wall.

6 Gargoyle A water spout carved to resemble a grotesque head.

7 Pier A solid masonry support; not necessarily a column.

8 Pinnacle A turret, or a tall ornament.

9 Rib A projecting moulding on the underside of an arched vault or ceiling, which may be ornamental or structured.

10 Spandrel A triangular space formed by an arch and the surrounding walls.

11 Tracery Masonry designs within a window.

12 Triforium An arched passage above the nave, transept or choir of a church.

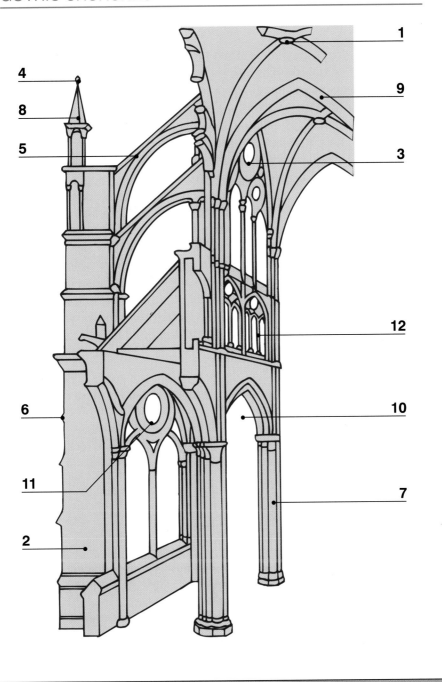

1
9
4
8
5
3
12
6
10
11
7
2

© DIAGRAM

EARLY-ENGLISH CHURCHES

This style marked the beginning of British Gothic. Records in the Domesday Book show that there were almost as many churches in England in 1086 as were recorded around 700 years later in a 1750s survey. Norman architects had encountered difficulties when creating intersections between aisles of different widths. Their Early-English successors solved these problems either by constructing pointed arches (the height of a pointed arch is not determined by its width), or by raising the level of the springers (the bottom stones) on the narrower semicircular arch. Churches after the 12th century had lighter, thinner structures with aisles and naves of varying widths. To support the increasingly high and thin walls, the flying buttress was introduced, which transferred the downward thrusts to supports away from the main inner wall. This allowed structures to have larger windows because the walls took less of the overall weight.

Features

1 Walls Thinner, lighter structures than Norman style and with increased window space. The first flying buttresses.

2 Windows Tall and set in groups with a thin, solid section above called 'plate tracery'. The beginning of the use of the pointed arch.

3 Doors Because of the use of pointed arches, the width of doors no longer needed to relate to the height of the arch. Entrances acquired a more graceful appearance.

4 Capitals Foliage and natural forms in deep relief.

5 Columns Circular or octagonal, with accompanying shafts.

6 Bases Simply set, on square or round footings.

7 Mouldings (**a**) Lively naturalistic elements; (**b**) regular repeat patterns of foliage.

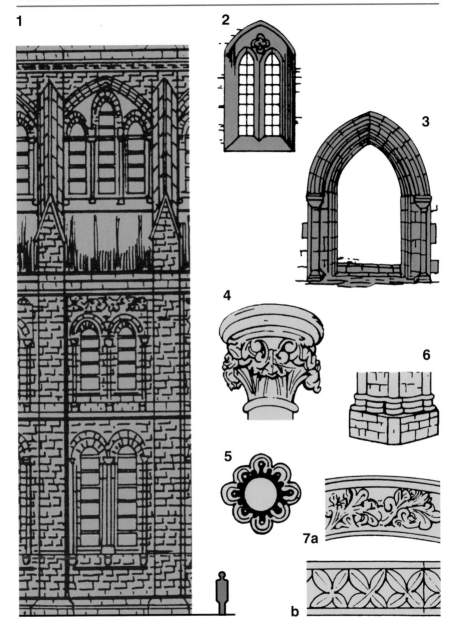

DECORATED CHURCHES

During the 14th century architects felt free to add decoration to all surfaces of their buildings. Advanced engineering skills were matched by ever greater sculptural qualities. The tracery within windows developed elaborate curves and great delicacy. Within existing buildings, delicately carved shrines and tombs were conceived like miniature buildings. Fonts, gargoyles, eagle lecterns, choir stalls and pulpits were also added to enrich interiors.

Features
1 Walls More and more of the wall space taken up with windows and tracery. Stage buttresses extend out from the walls, often with highly decorated steeple turrets.
2 Windows Larger windows resulted in the development of elaborate tracery, and the art of stained glass was taken to great heights.
3 Doors Often wide, with the newly developed ogee curve surround.
4 Capitals Simple, naturalistic foliage.
5 Columns Sometimes diamond-shaped or rectangular, but always deeply fluted.
6 Bases Square, but set at an angle to the line of the building.
7 Mouldings (**a**) Abstract versions of flowers; (**b**) other abstract patterns.

PERPENDICULAR CHURCHES

This style marked the culmination of British Gothic. It featured flatter, less pointed arches and the use of maximum window space. Repetitious vertical mouldings and fluting give interiors an illusion of heightened space which gave rise to the term 'perpendicular architecture'. A conspicuous feature was the elaborate interior roof decoration known as 'fan tracery'. After Henry VIII's dispute with Rome and the destruction of the monasteries, very little church building took place for 100 years. However, the perpendicular style continued to be used in domestic and civic architecture.

Typical buildings
King's College Chapel, Cambridge; St George's Chapel, Windsor; west front and nave, Winchester Cathedral; choir of York Minster; and tower and nave of Canterbury Cathedral.

Features
1 Walls Decorated with panelling that resembled window tracery. Also wide-reaching buttresses.
2 Windows The curved and straight arch, known as the four-centred arch, became the main feature on doors and windows and often occupied entire walls.
3 Doors The tops of doors appeared in the new window style, often with a protruding moulding.
4 Capitals Commonly polygonal in plan.
5 Columns Often groups of thin shafts set in diamond formations at frequent intervals along the side walls.

6 Bases Commonly polygonal in plan.
7 Mouldings These became less obtrusive, but with a simple directness of style. They featured: (**a**) natural foliage turned into geometric patterns; or (**b**) were modified into Tudor Roses, a symbol of Royal power.

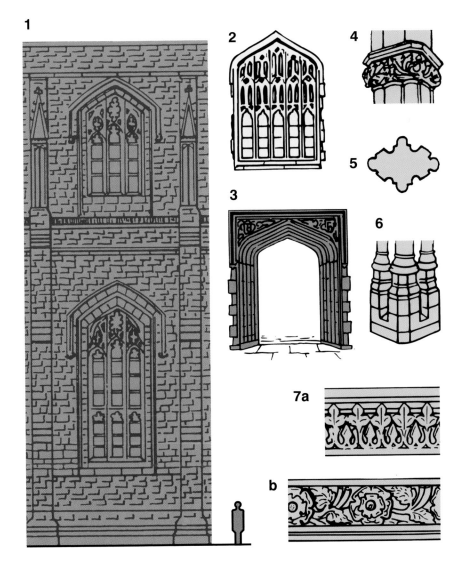

EXTERIOR PARTS OF A CHURCH

1 Bartizan A small turret projecting from a wall, parapet or tower.

2 Bellcote A bell tower on a roof.

3 Bell gable A bell tower mounted on the end wall.

4a Buttress A solid masonry support against a wall.

4b Flying buttress A support which is arched so that the brace is away from the wall.

5 Clerestory A row of windows in the upper part of a wall, above the roof of an aisle.

6 Finial An ornament on top of a building.

7 Fleche A small wooden spire.

8 Galilee An enclosed porch at the west end of a church.

9 Gargoyle A spout carrying water from the roof, usually decorated with a grotesque figure or head.

10 Lancet A tall and narrow pointed window.

11 Louvre A window opening, in a church tower, covered with overlapping boards.

12 Narthex A porch at the west end of a church.

13 Pinnacle A small stone spire on top of a buttress, parapet or roof.

14 Porch An entrance that is covered.

15 Rose window A circular window.

16 Spire A tall, pointed structure, most commonly found on top of a tower.

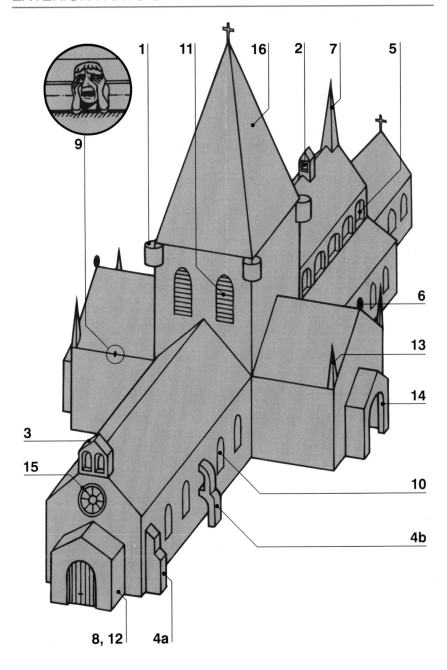

INTERIOR PARTS OF A CHURCH

1 Aisle The side corridors of the main church. The north aisle is on the left when facing the altar, and the south aisle is on the right.

2 Almonry A special room for the distribution of alms.

3 Ambulatory The continuation of the aisle around the choir and behind the altar.

4 Chancel The area containing the choir and the altar, originally reserved for the clergy.

5a Chapel A small area set aside for private worship.

5b Chantry chapel An endowed chapel in which prayers could be said for the soul of the benefactor.

5c Lady chapel Set at the east end and dedicated to the Virgin Mary.

6 Chapterhouse The administrative centre.

7 Choir The area between the nave and the altar, for use by the choir and clergy.

8 Cloister The covered walkway around a courtyard.

9 Crossing The central area between the nave, the chancel and the transept.

10 Crypt The area under the main church (not shown on the plan).

11 Nave The main area of the church used by the congregation. It usually has aisles on either side.

12 Presbytery The area around the main altar.

13 Sacristy A room for storing the priests' vestments and sacred vessels.

14 Sanctuary The most sacred part of the chancel. It provided fugitives from the law with immunity from arrest.

15 Slype A passageway from cloister to transept or chapterhouse.

16 Transept The two areas on either side of the crossing, which form part of the cross-shaped plan of the church.
17 Vestry Another term for the sacristy, where vestments and sacred vessels are kept.

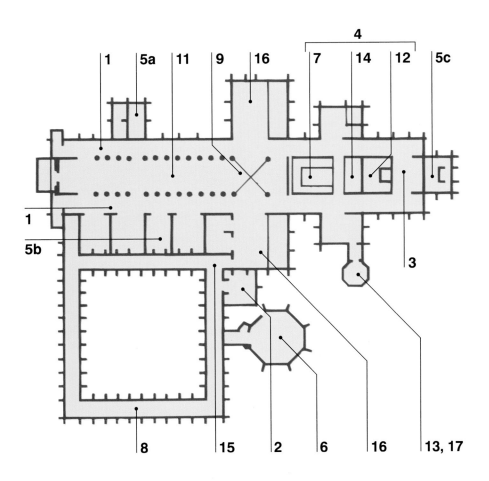

CHURCH FURNISHINGS

1 Altar The table at the east end of the church from which acts of worship are conducted.

2 Brasses Engraved brass plates attached to tombs. They usually depict the deceased.

3 Canopy A protective hood over a pulpit or tomb.

4 Choir screen The partition, usually of wood, between the choir stalls and the nave of the church.

5 Credence A small table or shelf for the bread and wine used in a Communion service.

6 Easter sepulchre A recess in the north chancel which holds an effigy of the risen Christ during Easter.

7 Font A large raised basin containing holy water; used for baptisms.

8 Funeral hatchments Lined with wooden painted shields, called 'hatchments', bearing the arms of deceased local gentry.

9 Lectern A desk or stand designed to hold a bible or large service book.

10 Misericord A seating ledge, often decorated and carved. Built to support a person without a pew during a long church service.

11 Pew Wooden seating for the congregation.

12 Piscina A stone basin near the altar, used for washing the sacred vessels.

13 Pulpit An elevated platform, reached by a flight of steps, from which the congregation is addressed.

14 Reredos A decorated screen behind the altar.

15 Rood A cross or crucifix placed in the east part of the nave and in front of the choir stalls.

16 Roodscreen The support to the rood, often elaborately carved in wood or stone.

17 Screen A screen surrounding an altar or shrine.

18 Sedilia Seats for the clergy, often recessed.

19 Squint A small slit in the wall or pier that enabled members of the congregation (usually lepers in a separate room) to see the altar.
20 Stall Another name for a pew.
21 Stoup A basin of holy water near the church entrance.

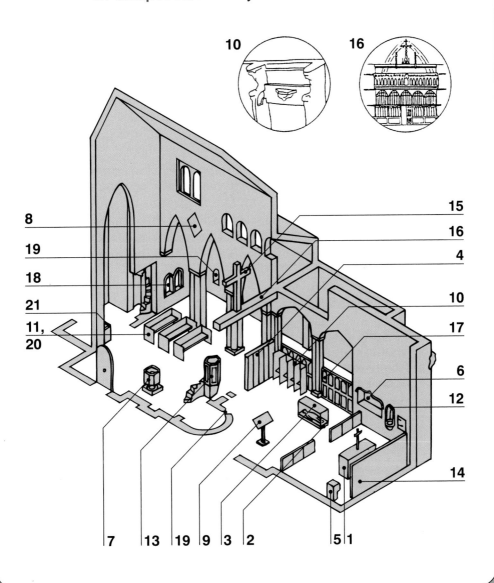

© DIAGRAM

Castles

DEVELOPMENT OF THE CASTLE

From the earliest times homesteads were defended by a
wooden fence (or palisade) which stood on top of a
mound surrounded by a ditch. Nearby trees and
undergrowth would have been cleared to make a secret
approach difficult and, if possible, the ditch would have
been flooded. The area within the encirclement (called
the bailey) would have contained assorted domestic,
agricultural and military buildings including kennels,
stables, an armoury, a workshop, a brewhouse, a
bakehouse and a chapel. In times of siege, neighbouring
farmers would bring their livestock into the bailey for
protection in exchange for taking up arms in defence of
their fuedal lord. Defences developed first from simple
encampments around a keep (the lord's residence). Later,
strong gatehouses and, finally, a small hill (a motte), on
which the keep was built, were added.

1 Keep and bailey castles Until the 11th century, the
keep was usually a wooden structure.
2 Gatehouse and bailey castle Placing greater
emphasis on the outer wall and gateway was a more
likely way to ensure good defence.
3 Motte and bailey castle By the 11th century, local
barons preferred motte and bailey castles. The motte is a
high mound either fashioned from the landscape or man-
made. The keep surmounting the motte would have been
of timber. Later, wooden structures were replaced with
solid stone.

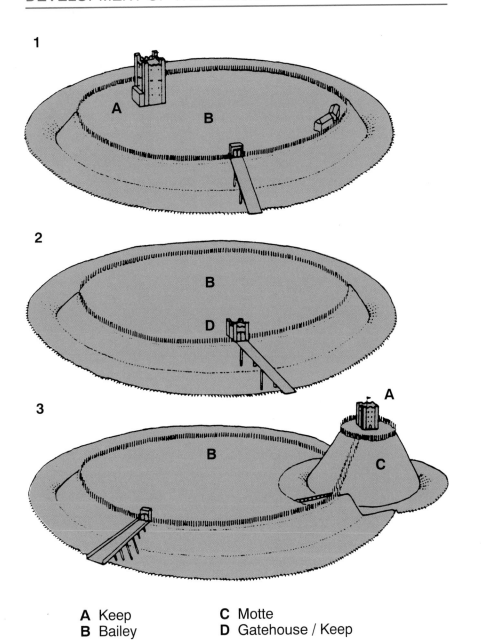

1

2

3

A Keep
B Bailey
C Motte
D Gatehouse / Keep

PARTS OF A CASTLE

1 Angle tower Positioned on corners, enabling archers to cover two sides of a castle.

2 Arrow slits Narrow openings in the wall through which archers could shoot at attackers.

3 Bastion An individual turret or tower on a wall.

4 Causeway The paved approach to a castle entrance.

5 Crenellated walls The protruding walls provided archers with cover, whilst the gaps inbetween afforded them an opportunity to shoot at attackers.

6 Drawbridge An entrance platform over a ditch or moat which could be raised when under attack.

7 Flanking tower Protruding from the walls, they enabled archers to provide cover along the castle walls.

8 Garderobe A medieval lavatory.

9 Gatehouse Defences over a gate.

10 Inner bailey The area closest to the keep, usually separated from the outer bailey by an inner ring of defensive walls.

11 Keep The strongest building in a castle.

12 Machicolation holes Through which defenders could shoot arrows, drop stones or pour boiling oil on attackers.

13 Moat Usually a man-made ditch flooded with water.

14 Outer bailey The area outside the inner defences protected by the outer ramparts.

15 Outer curtain wall The outermost wall, usually linking turrets (bastions).

16 Palisade A wooden defensive wall.

17 Portcullis A heavy gate or grill which could be lowered when a castle was under attack.

18 Postern gate (Sally Port) A small, secret exit away from the main gate.

19 Ramparts Defensive walls or castle battlements.

20 Scarp Steeply sloping land at the foot of the battlements.

21 Watchtower The tallest turret on a keep or wall.

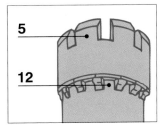

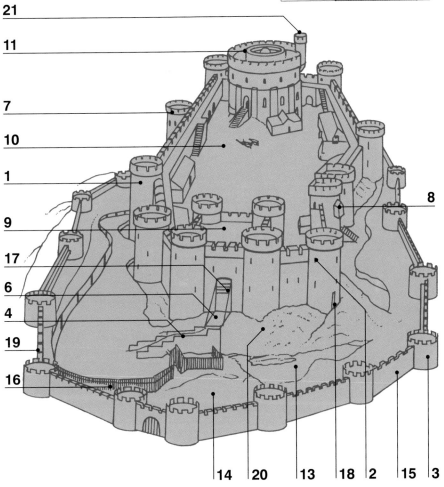

Unusual Buildings

1 Dovecote A building to house pigeons. This medieval example is at Daylingworth, Gloucestershire.

2 Field house A stone building usually set on moorland and used to house sheep in winter.

3 Folly A monument built for the amusement of the owner. This example was erected in 1840 and stands 52 m (170 ft) high.

4 Lichgate A covered gate at the entrance to a churchyard.

1

3

2
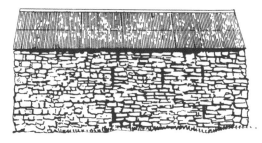

4

5 Lighthouse A coastal tower with lights to warn approaching ships of dangers. This is Eddystone Lighthouse, off Plymouth in Devon; it was built in 1759.

6 Mausoleum A building containing the remains of a local dignitary. This one was built in 1854 in Strathclyde, for Alexander, 10th Duke of Hamilton.

7 Pumping station A tower containing a raised water tank and water pump. This 19th century example is in London.

8 Quoit The stone remains of neolithic (2000 BC) tombs, also called 'dolmen' or 'chromlech'. This example is in Cornwall.

5

7

6

8

© DIAGRAM

9 Tithe barn A large barn erected to store the tithe – a tax paid in the form of cereals by tenants of ecclesiastical lands. This 14th century example is in Glastonbury, Somerset.

10 Toll house The home of a toll keeper who collected fees (tolls) from passing traffic. Many toll houses were built in the 18th century.

11 Watch box Sentinel boxes built in the 18th century to guard cemeteries from body-snatchers.

12 Well house A covering for a well supplying water to surrounding buildings. This medieval example is in West Sussex.